Moron

GARDEN SWEAR

Wondrous Swear Word To Color

For Stress Releasing

Charity Borsberry

I0463940

Happy Coloring!

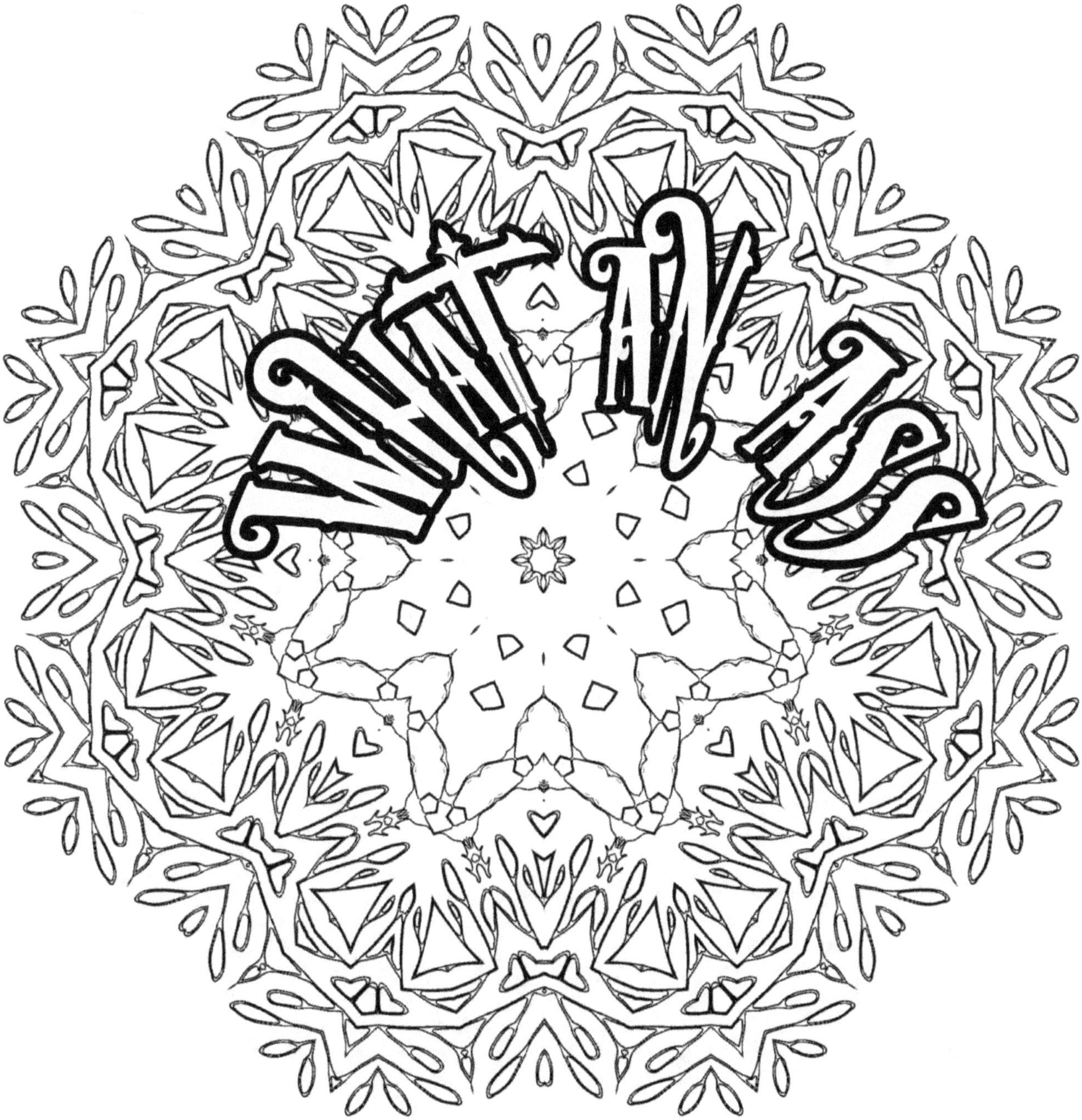
WHAT AN ASS

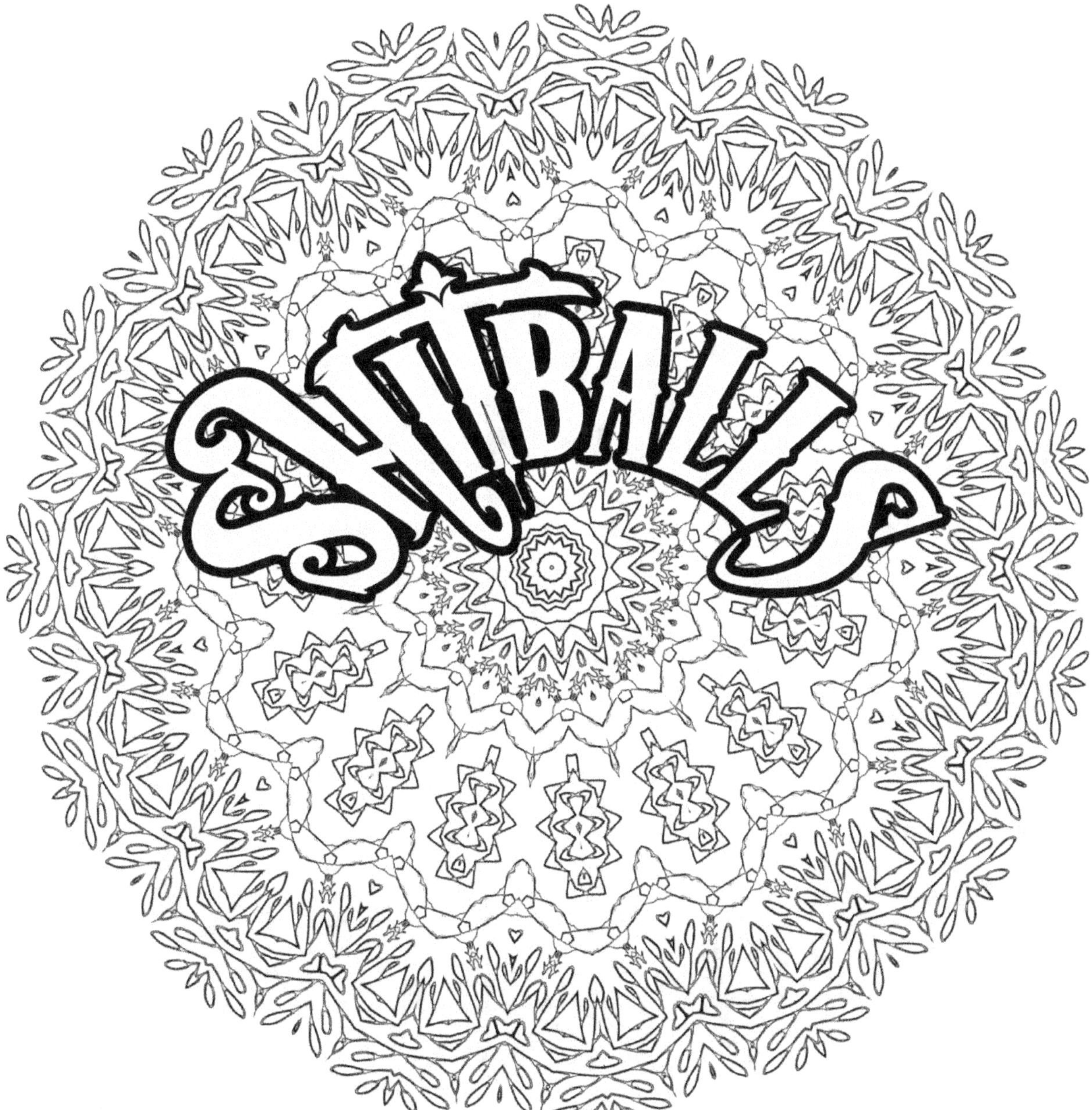

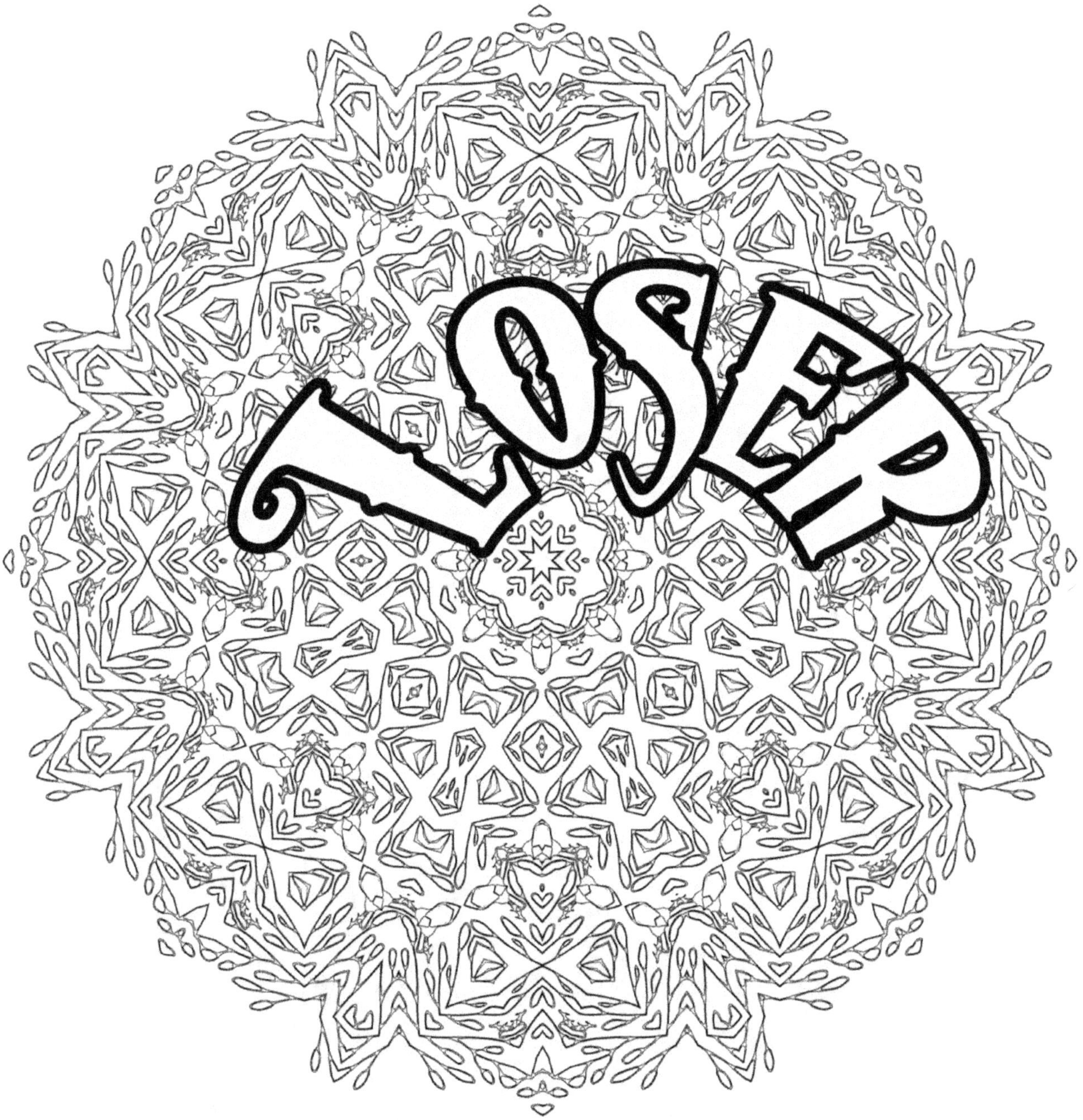
LOSER

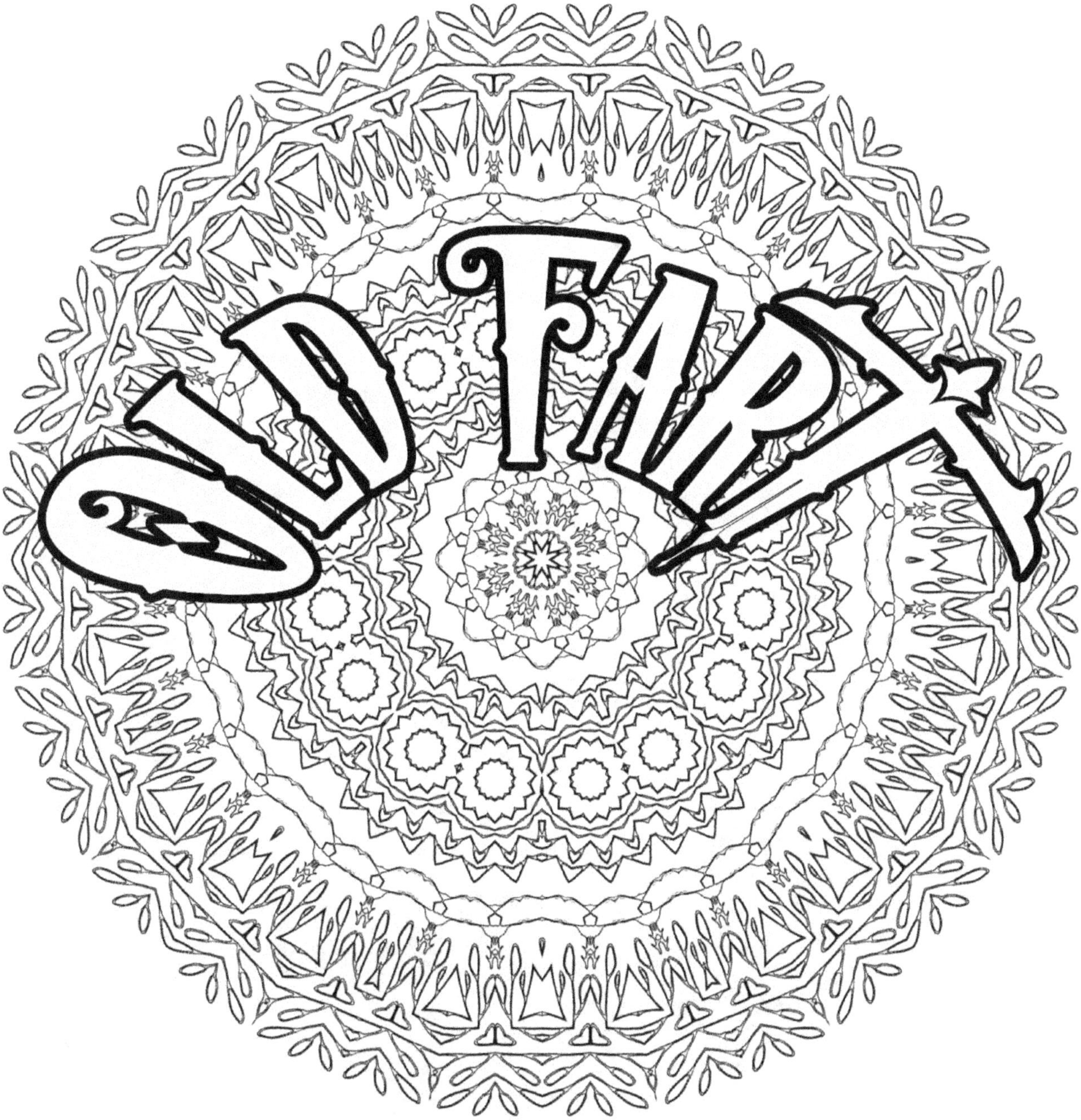
OLD FART

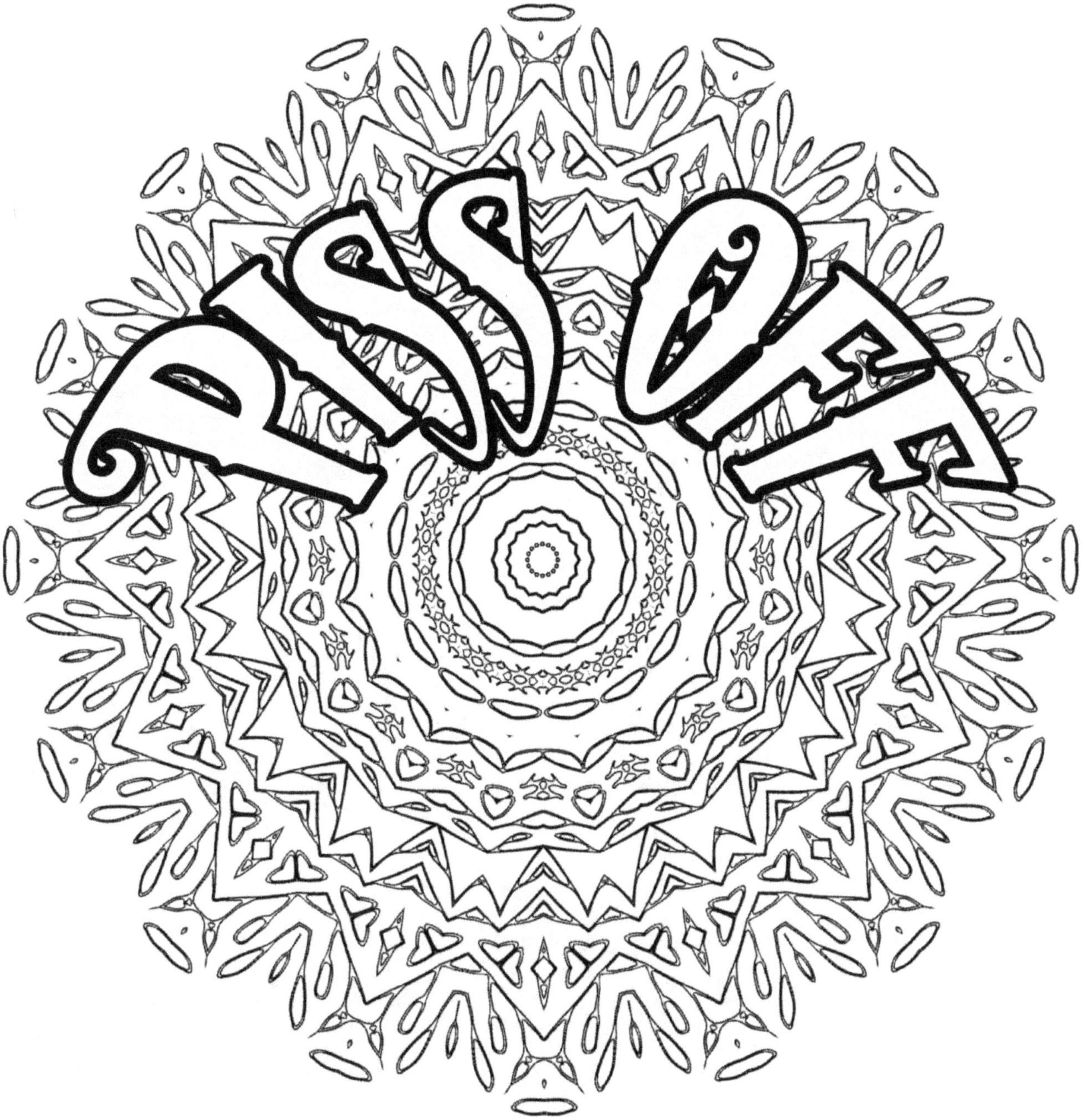
PISS OFF

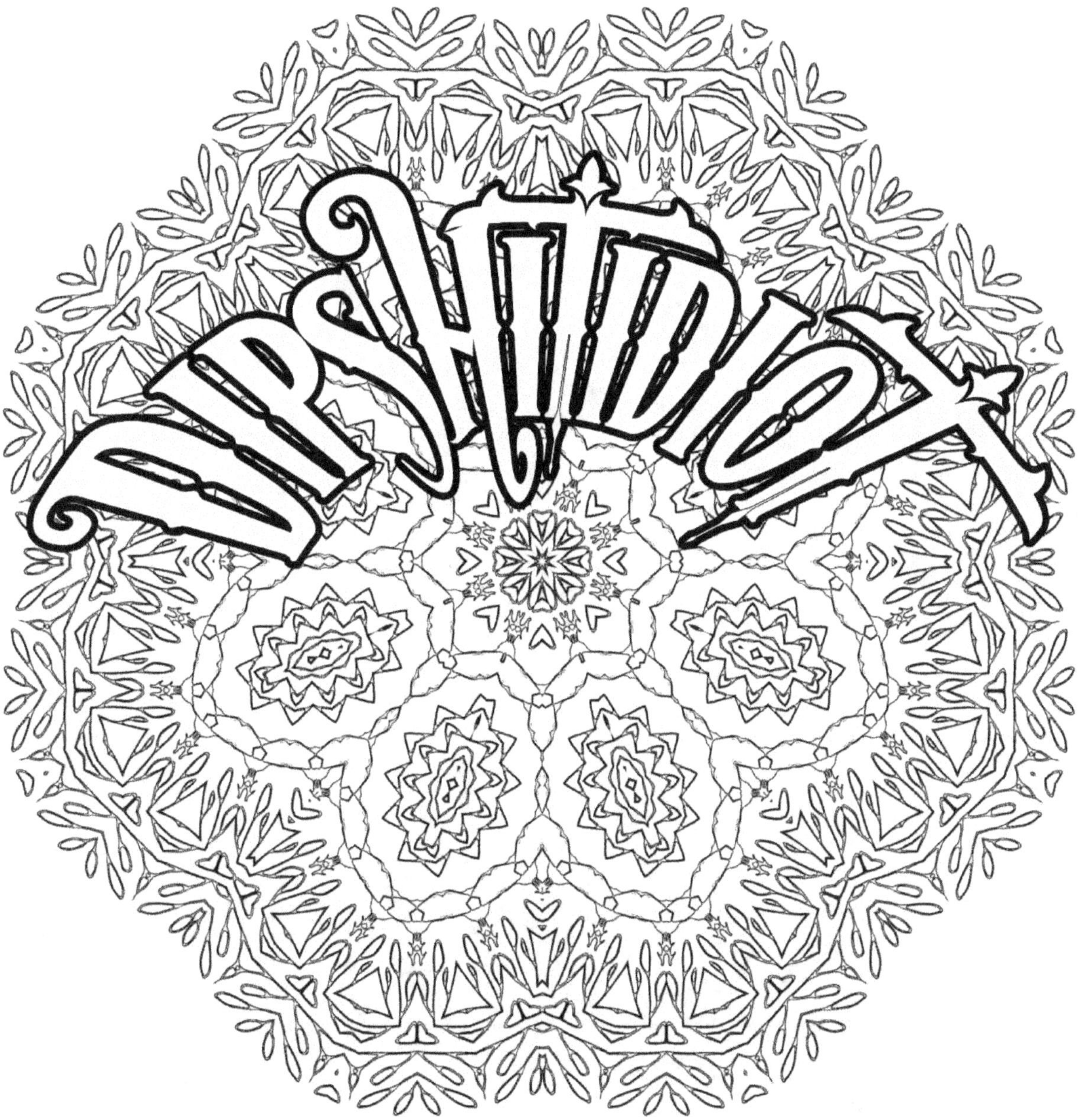
DIPSHITIDIOT

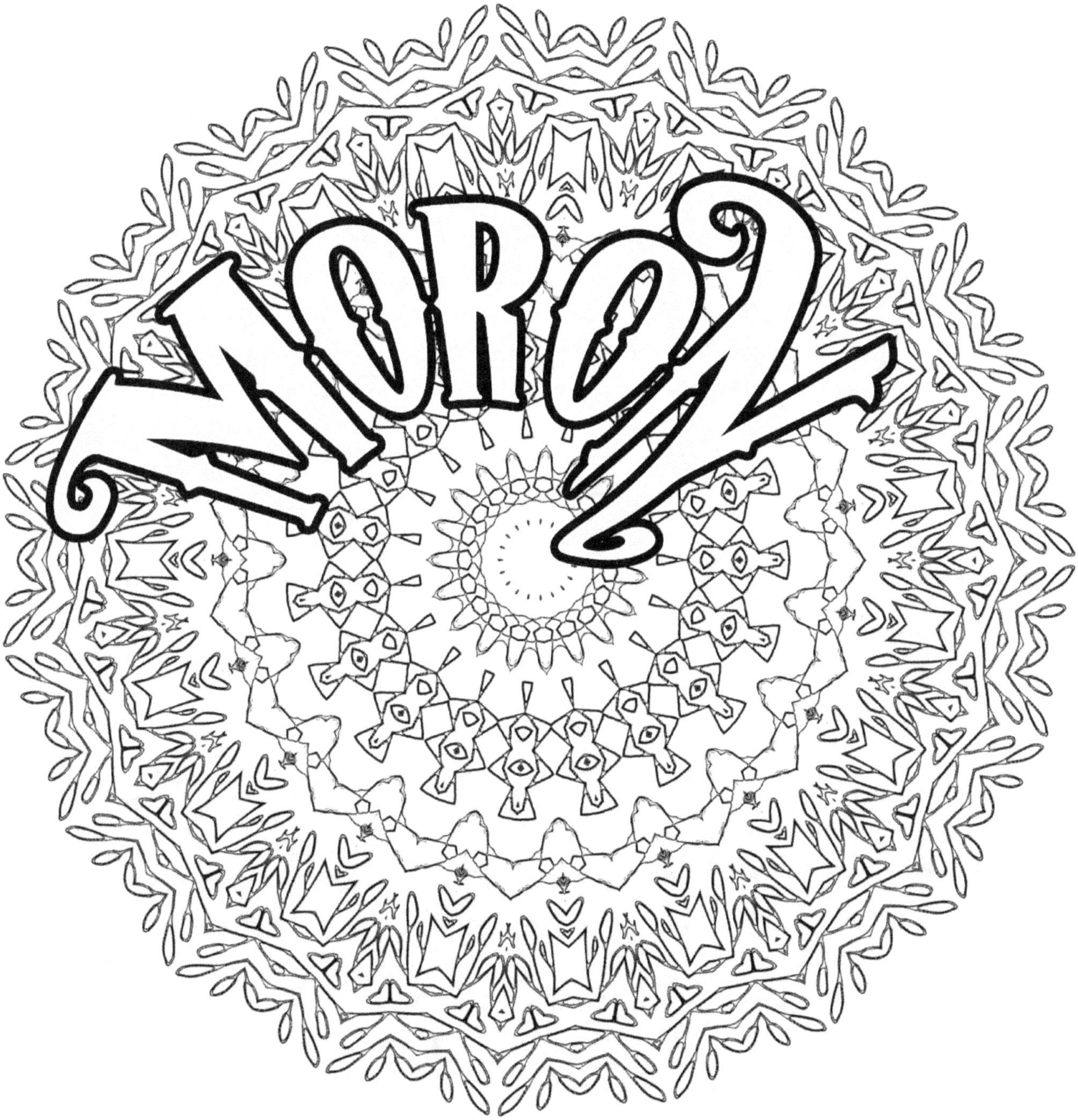

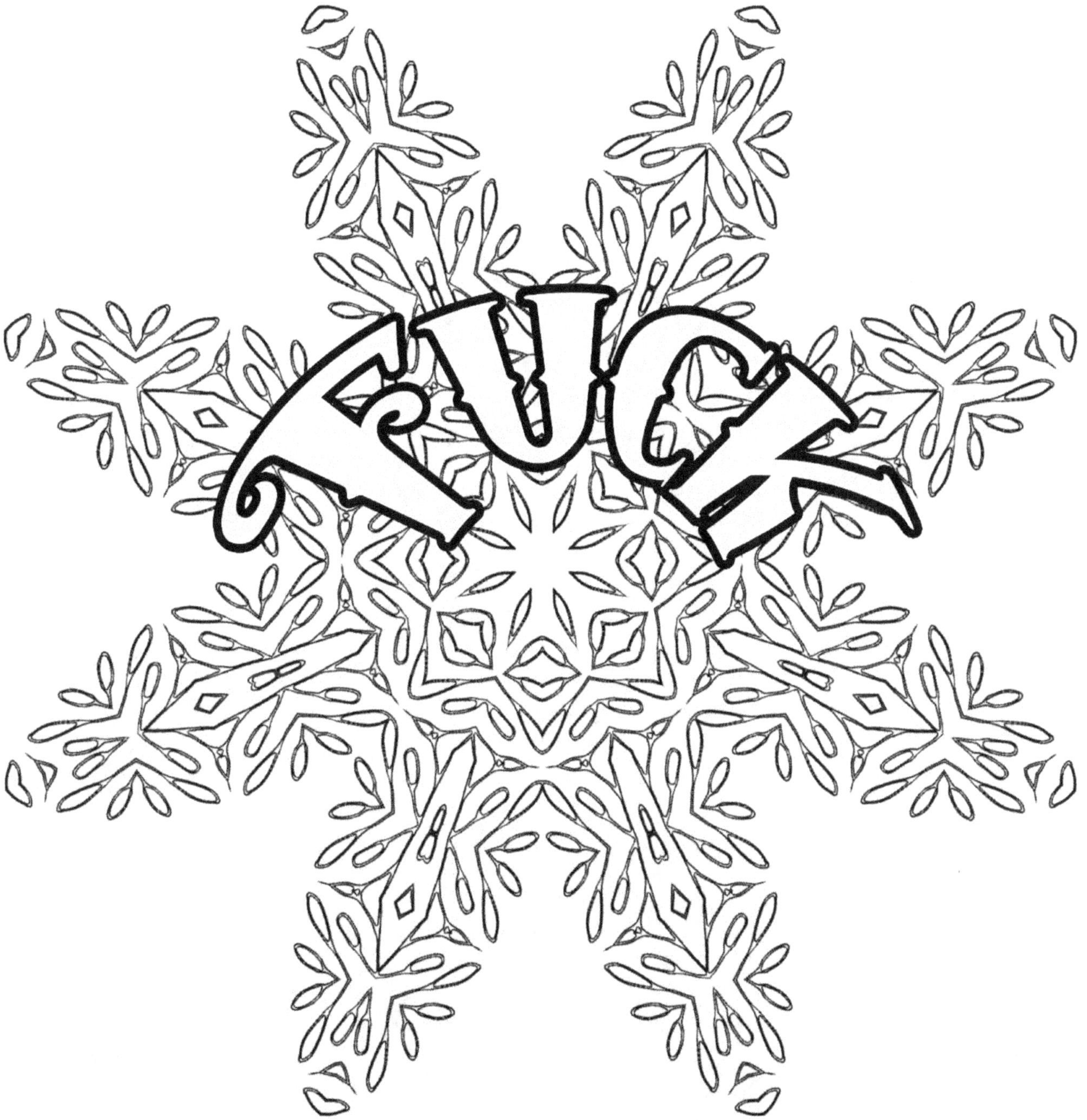
FUCK

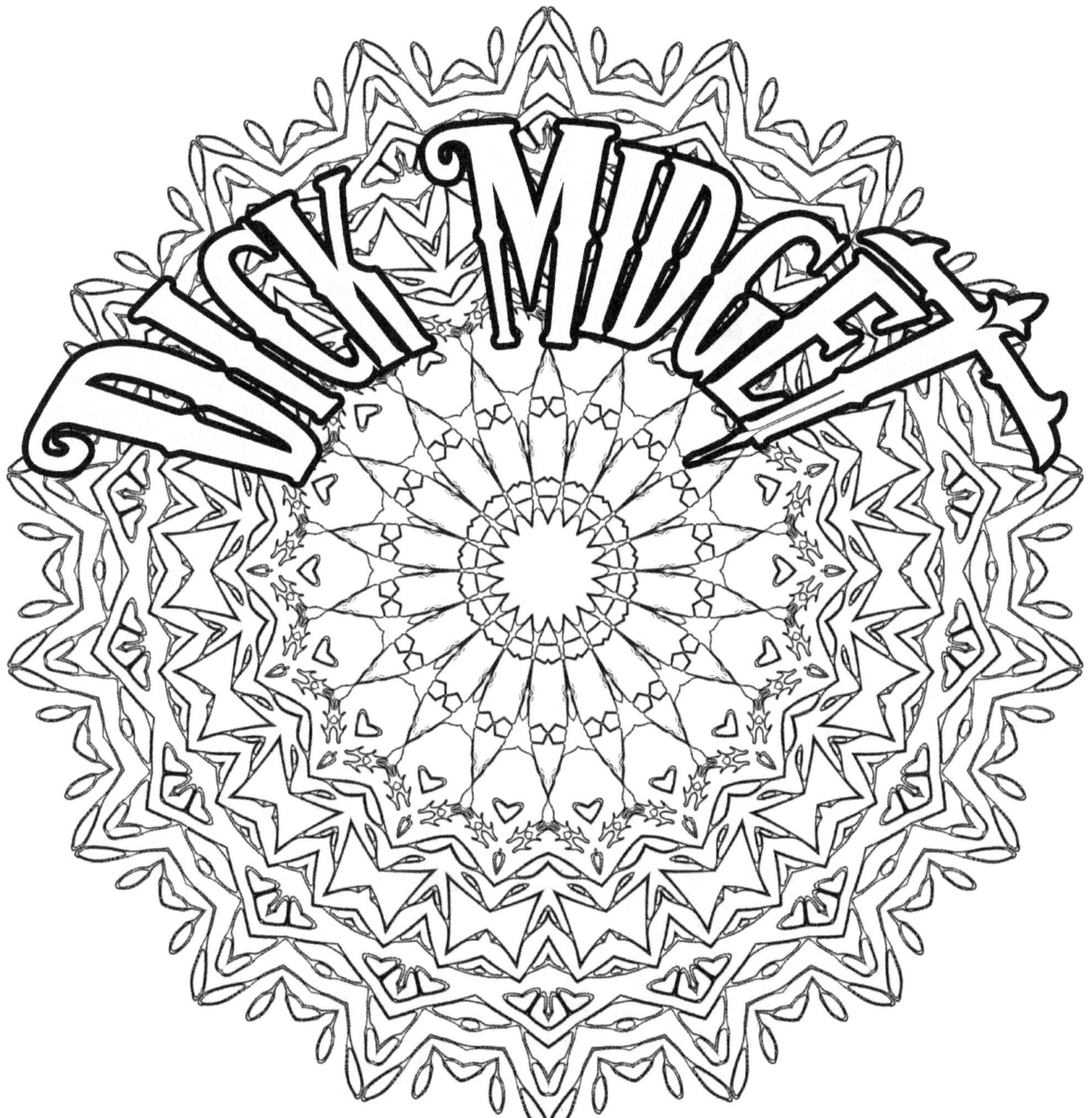
DICK MIDGET

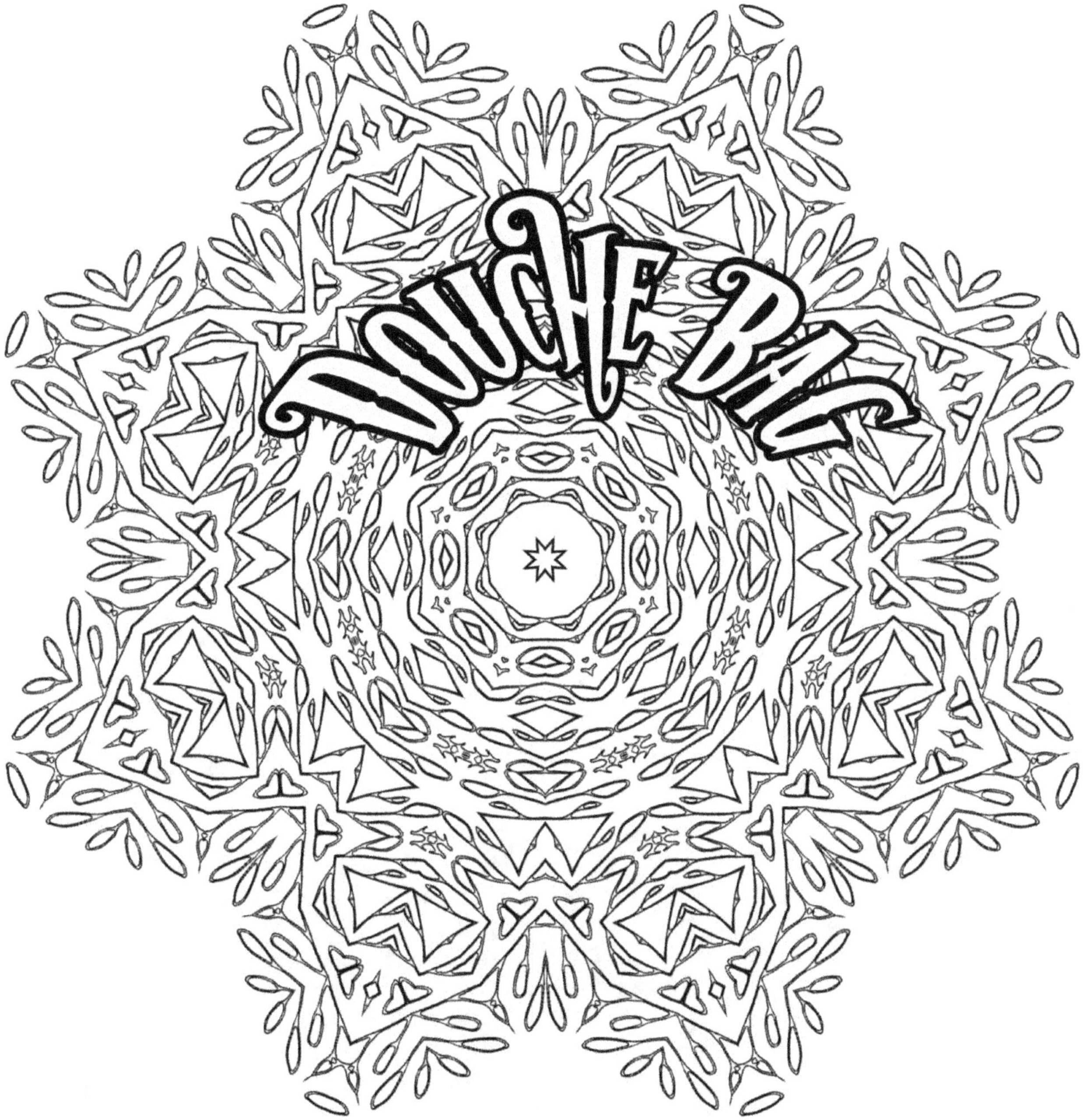
DOUCHE BAG

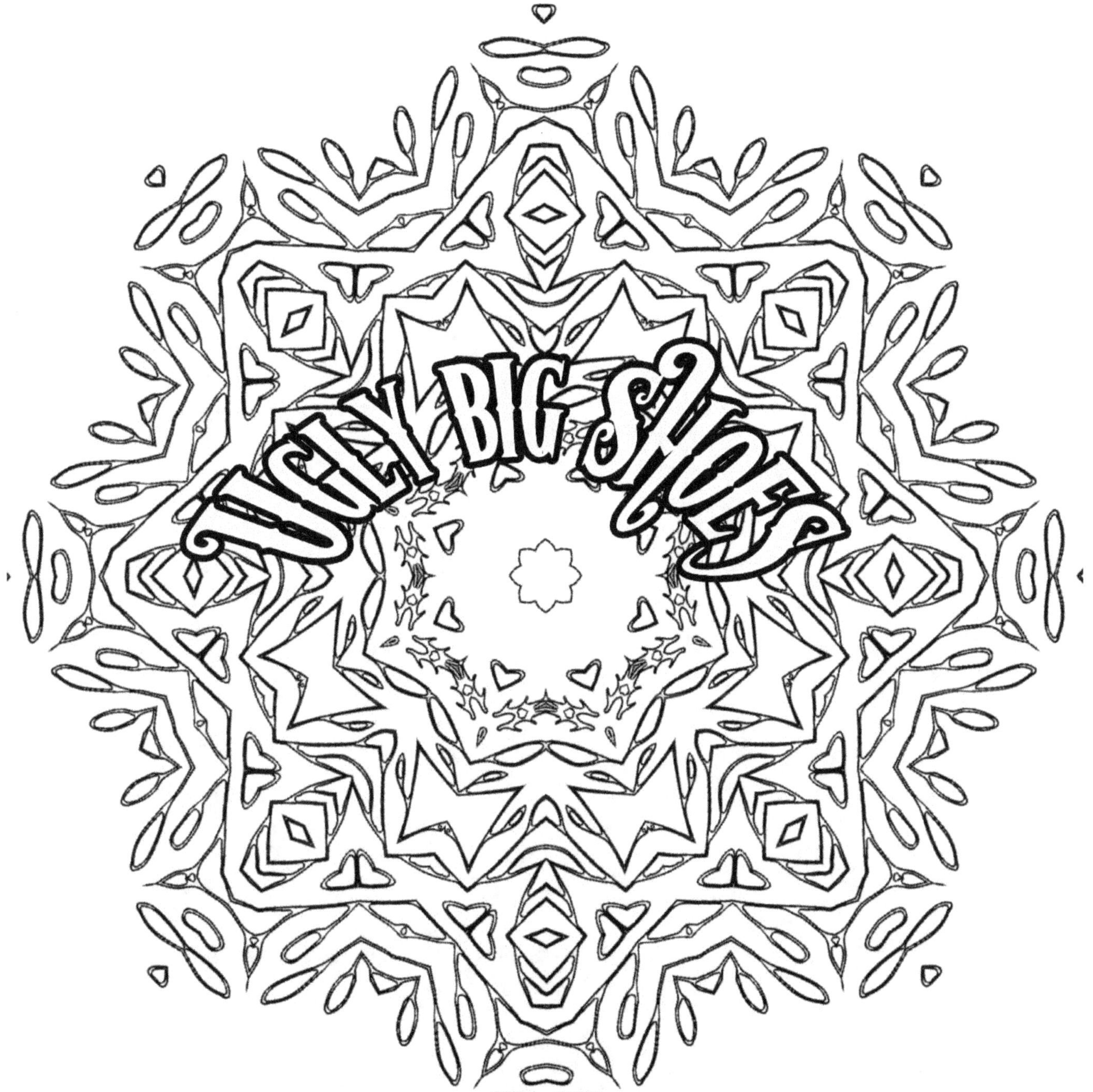
UGLY BIG SHOES

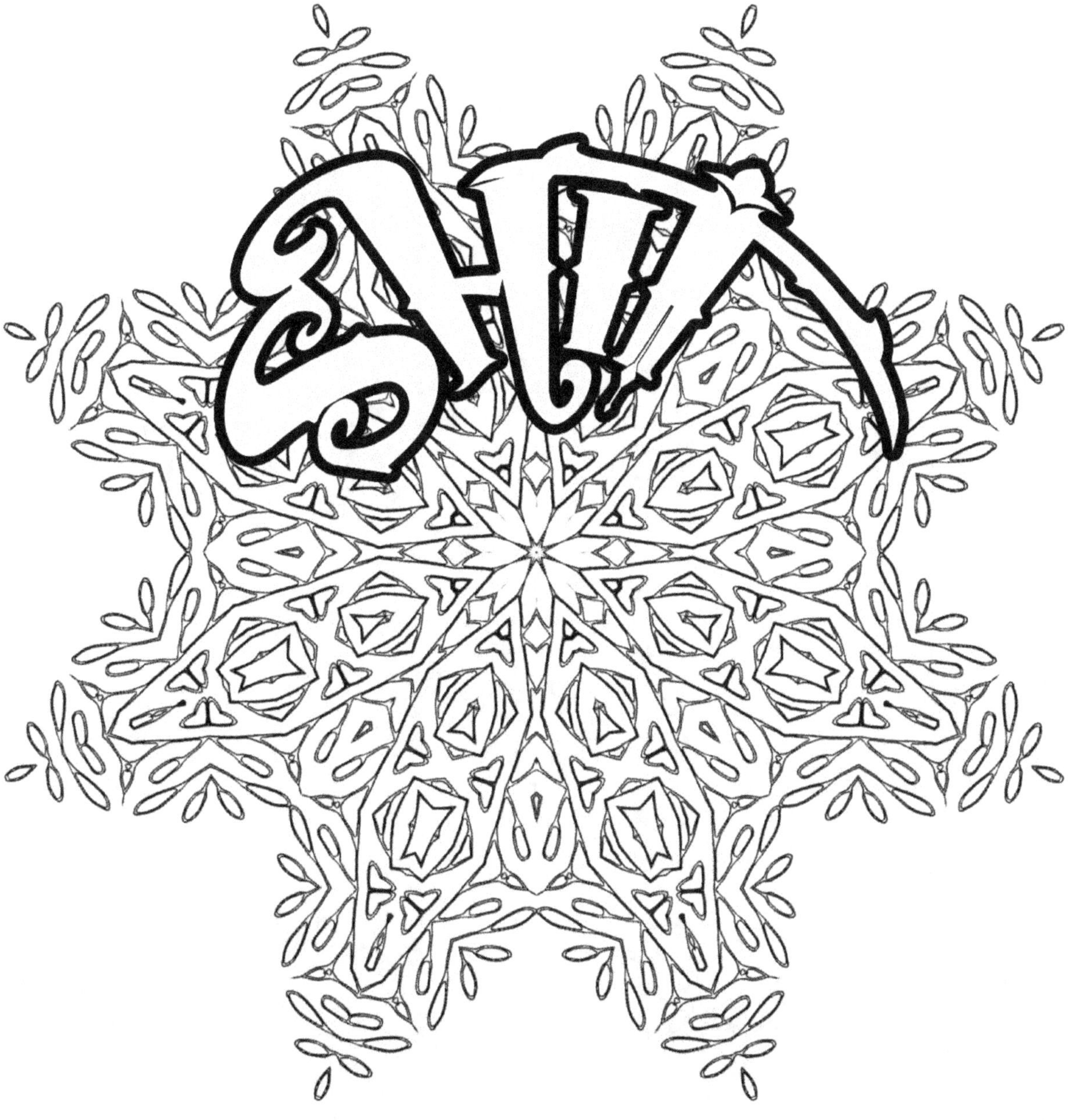
SHIT

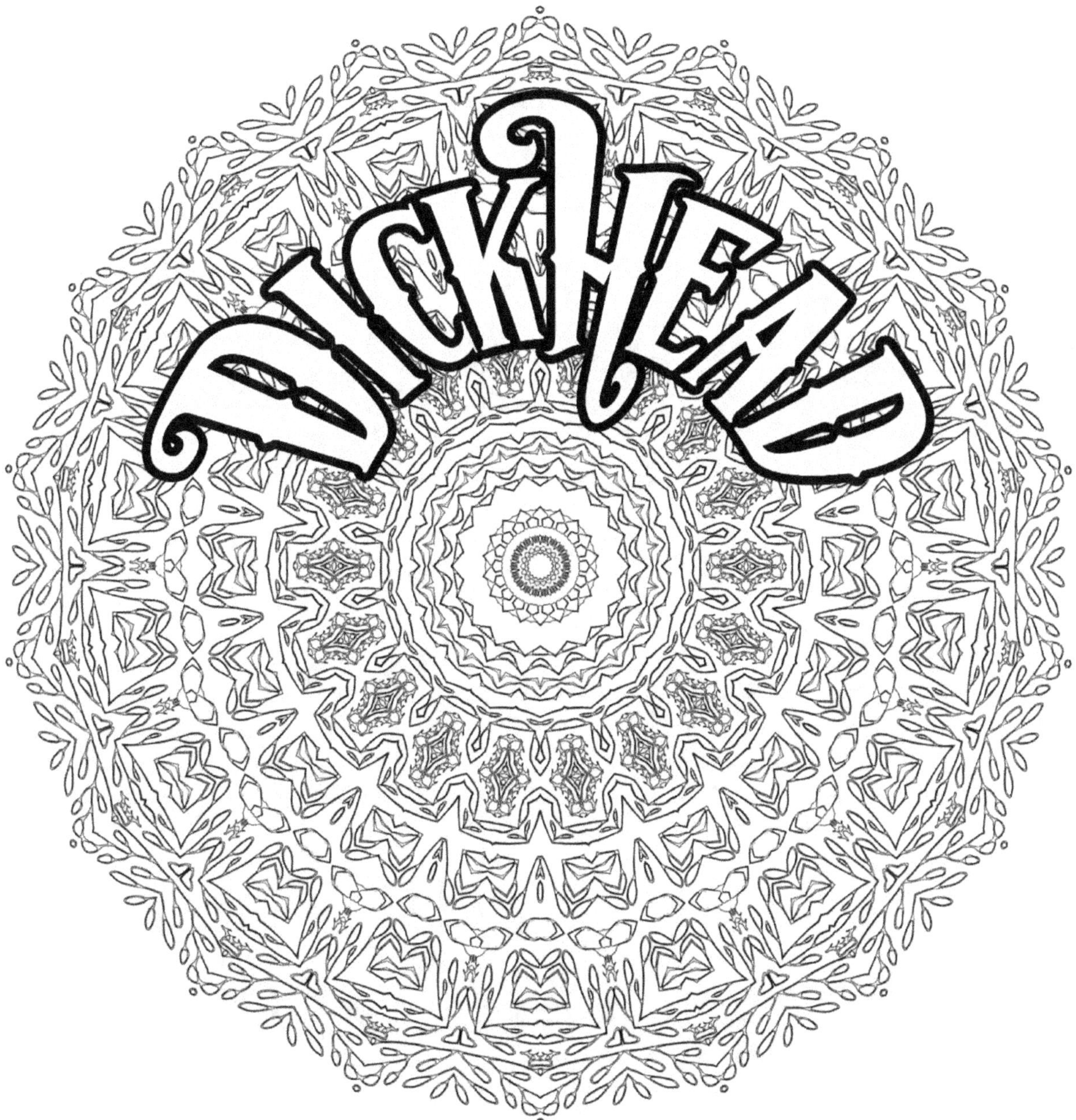
DICKHEAD

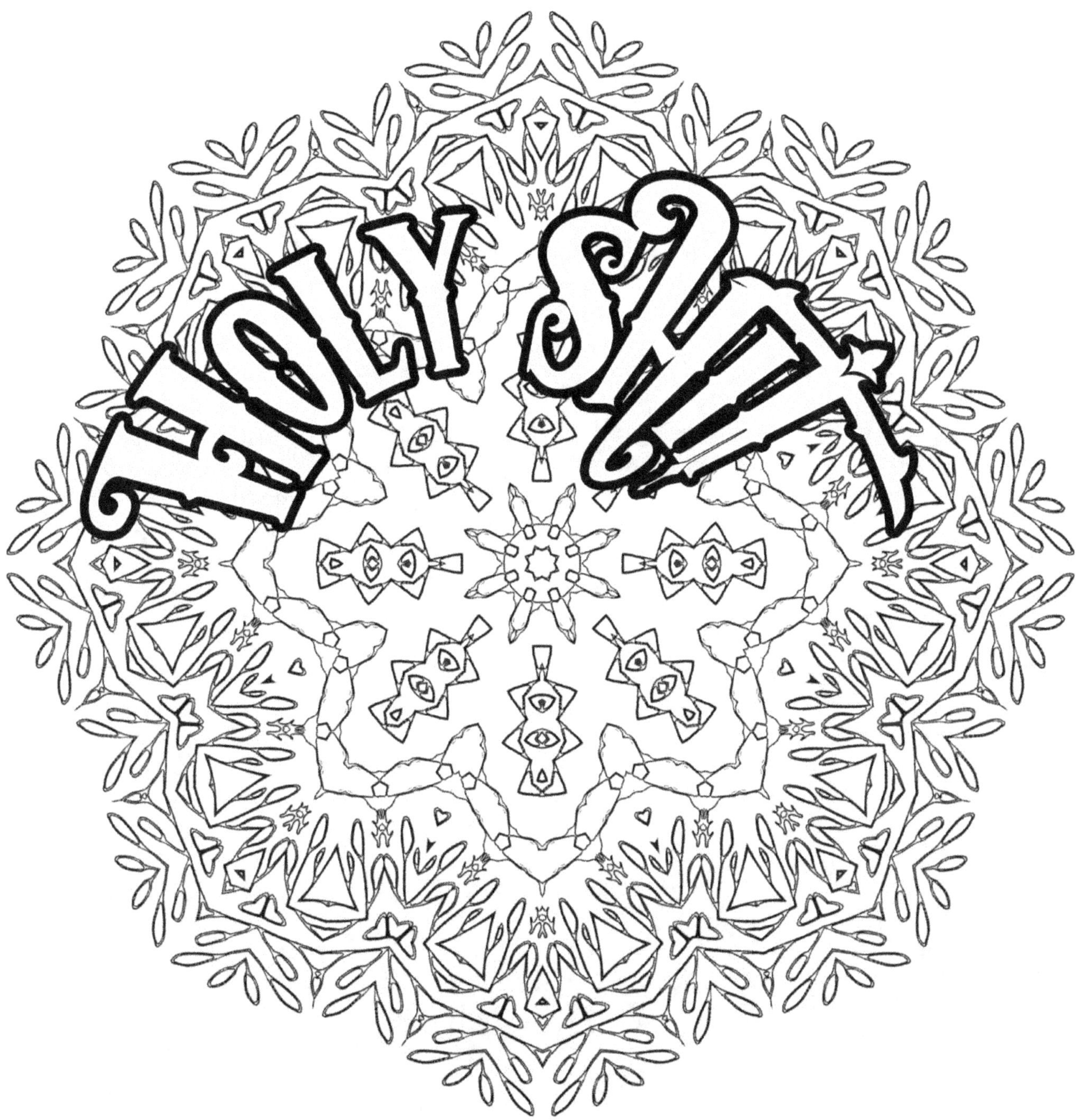
HOLY SHIT

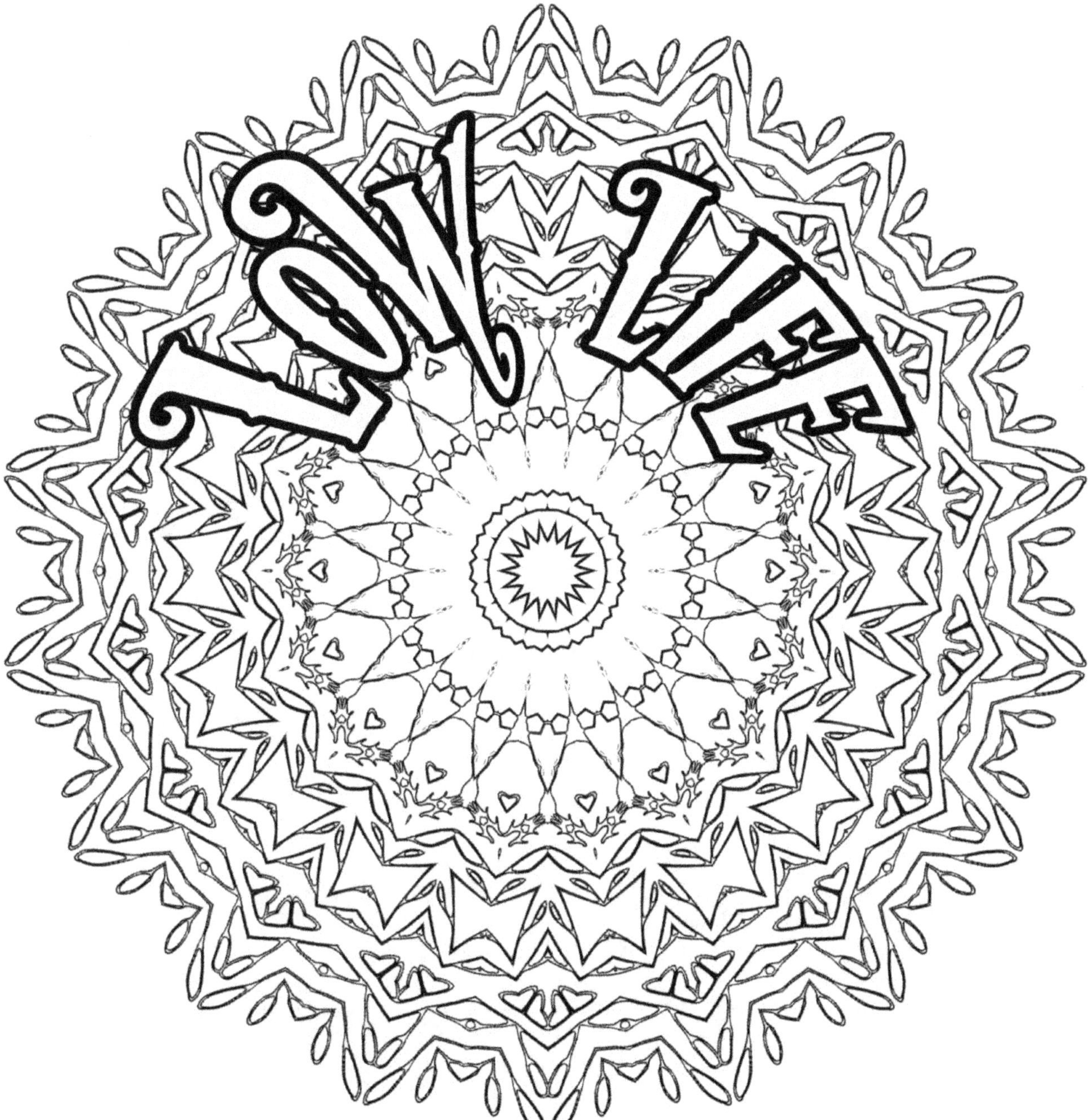
LOW LIFE

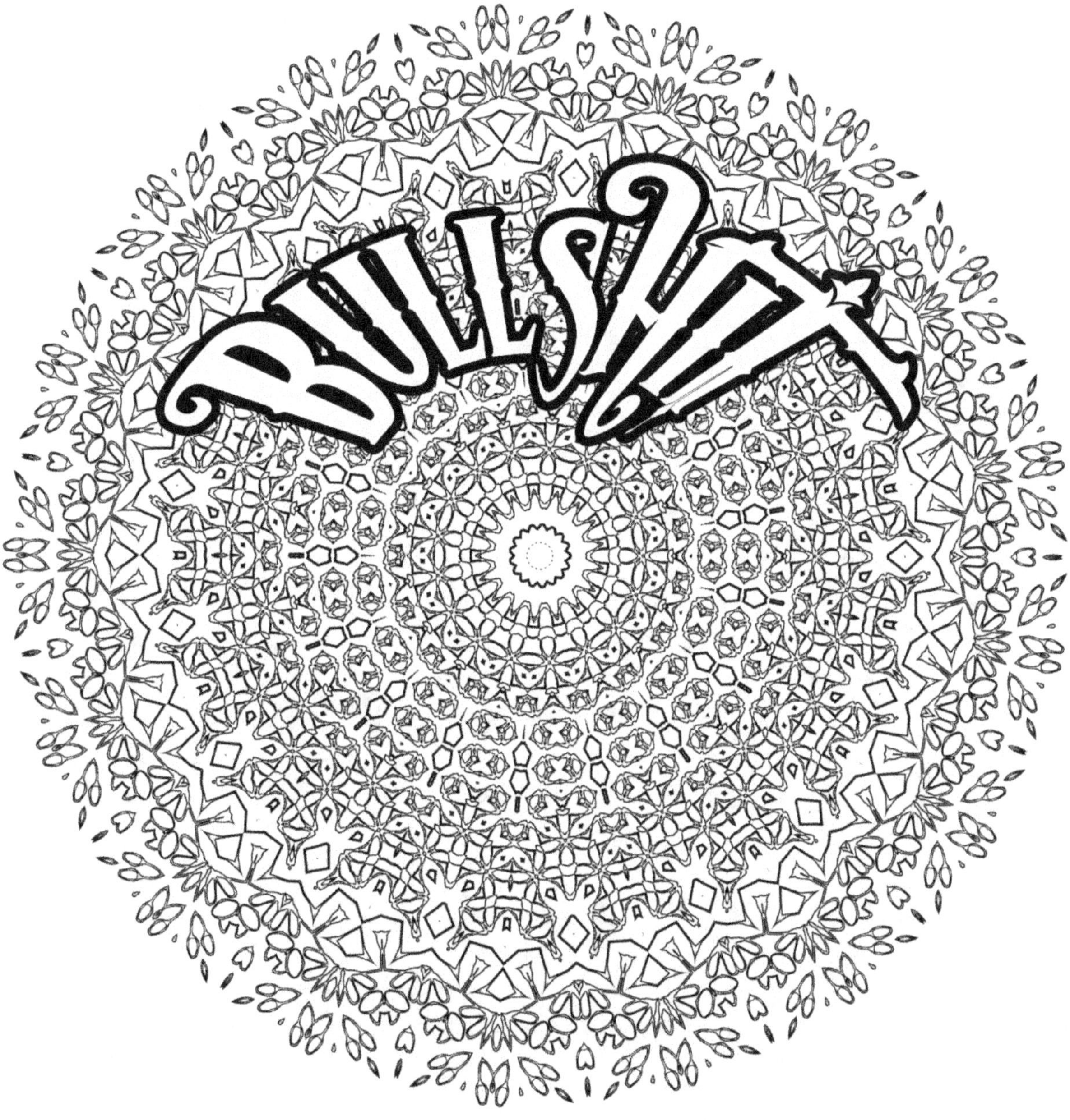
BULLSHIT

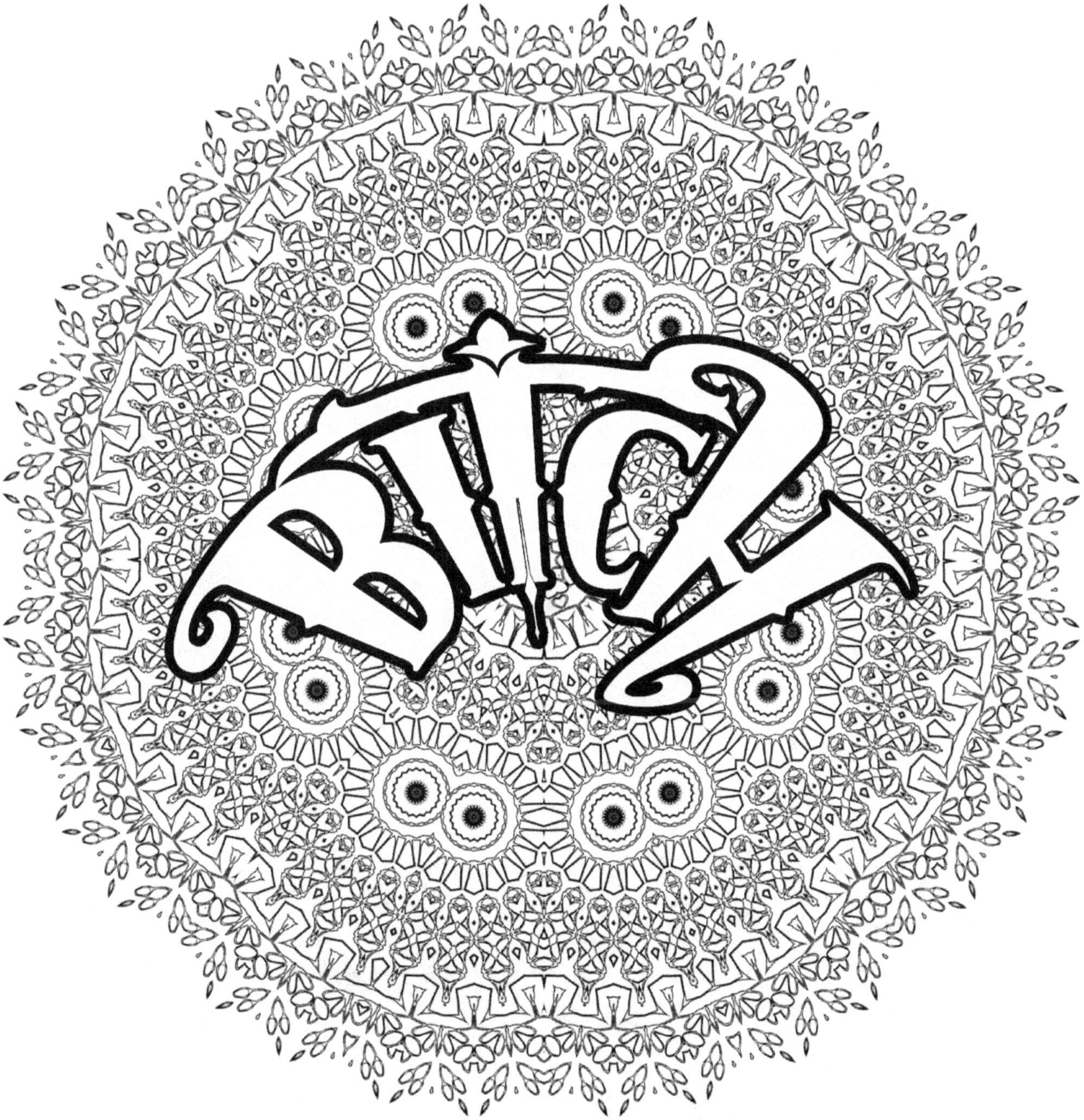
BITCH

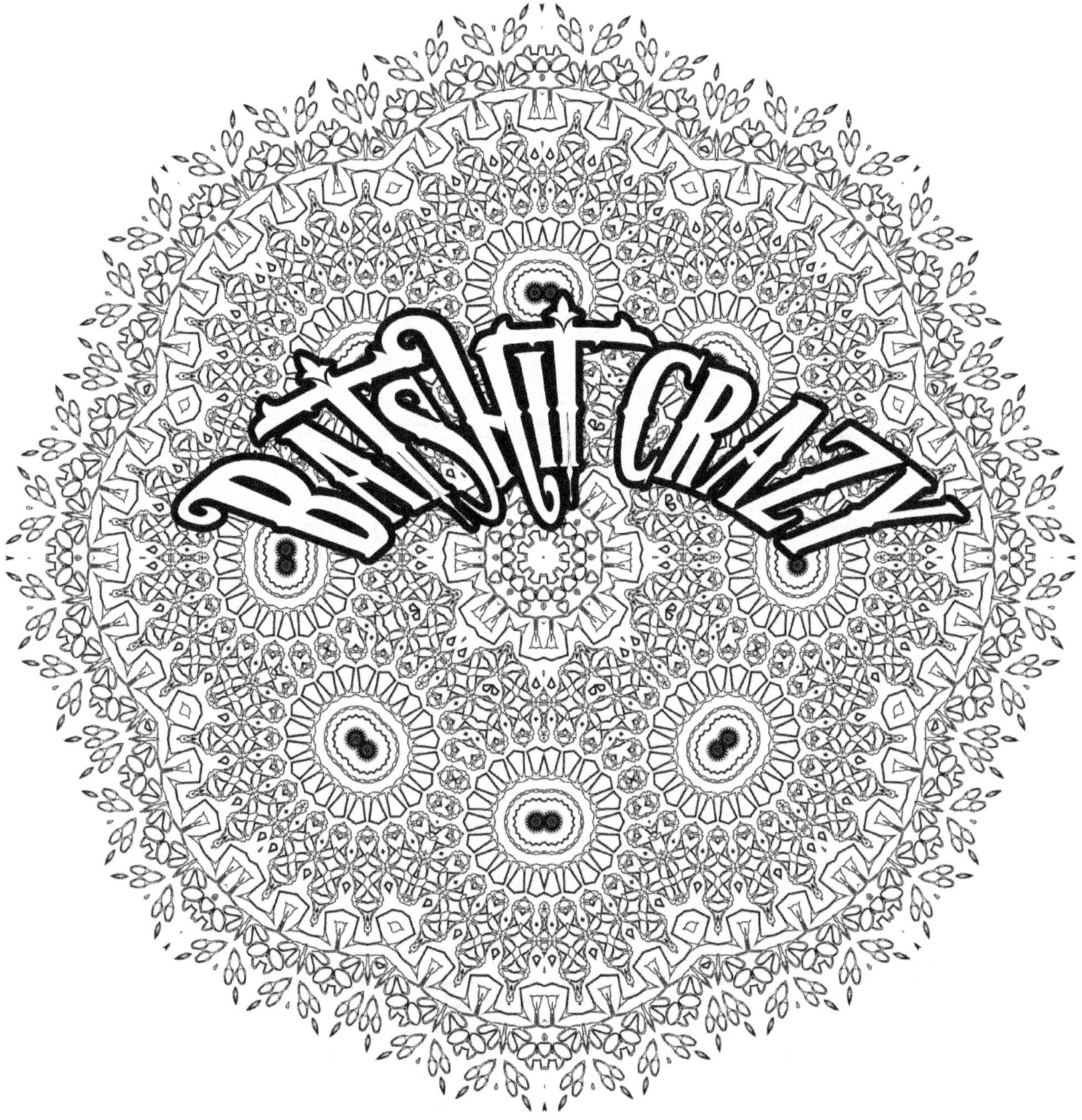
BATSHIT CRAZY

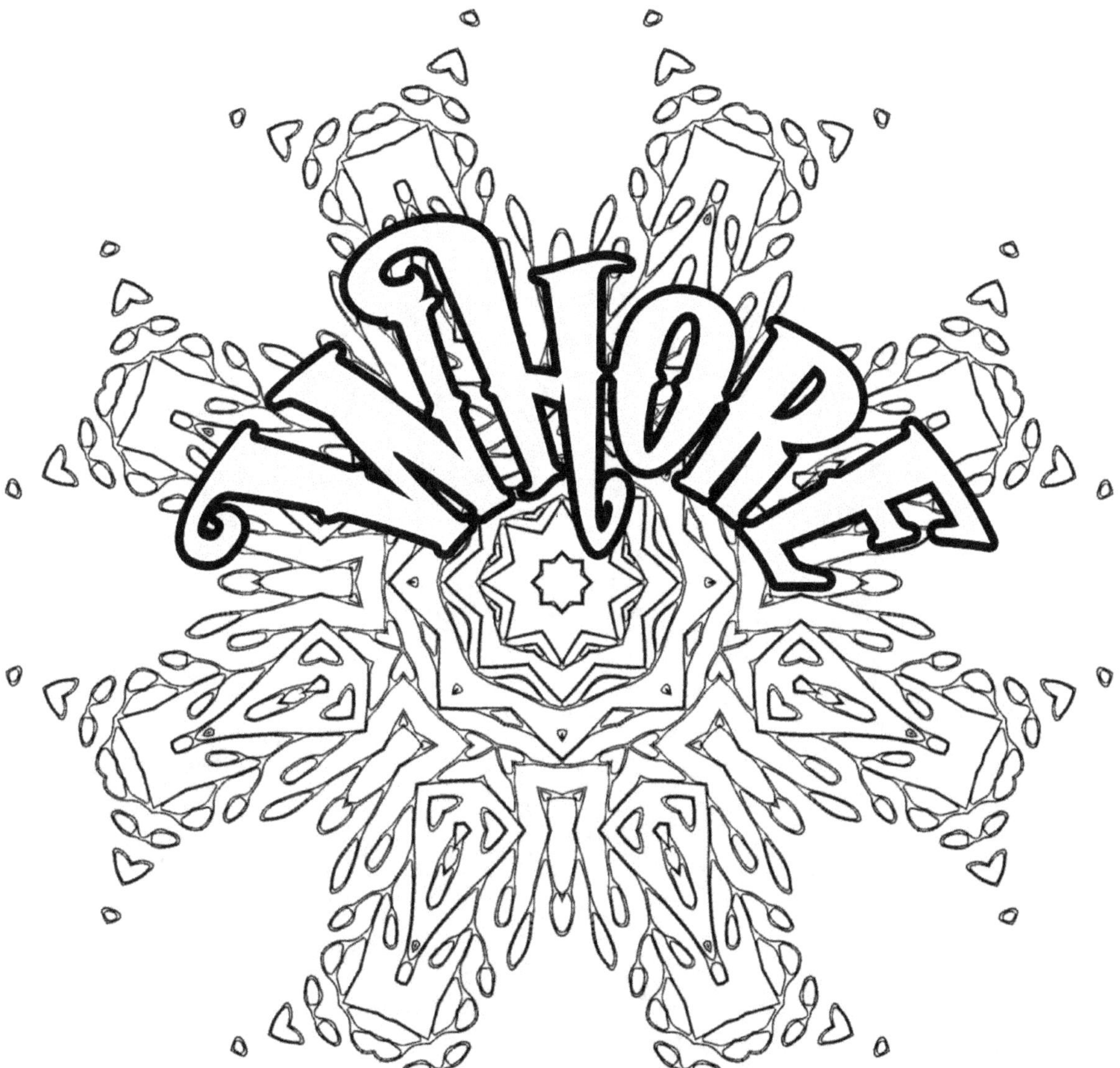
WHORE

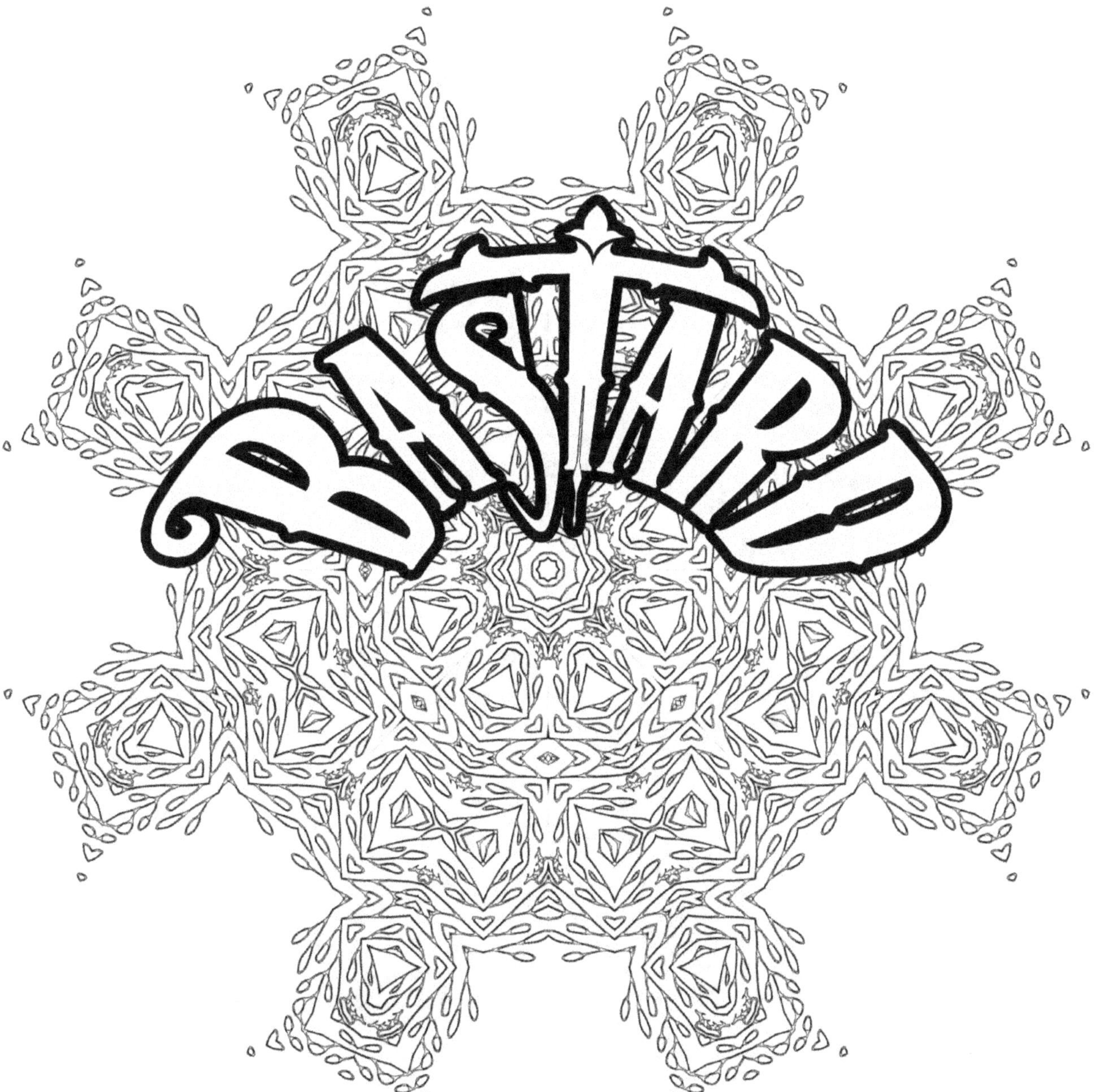
BASTARD

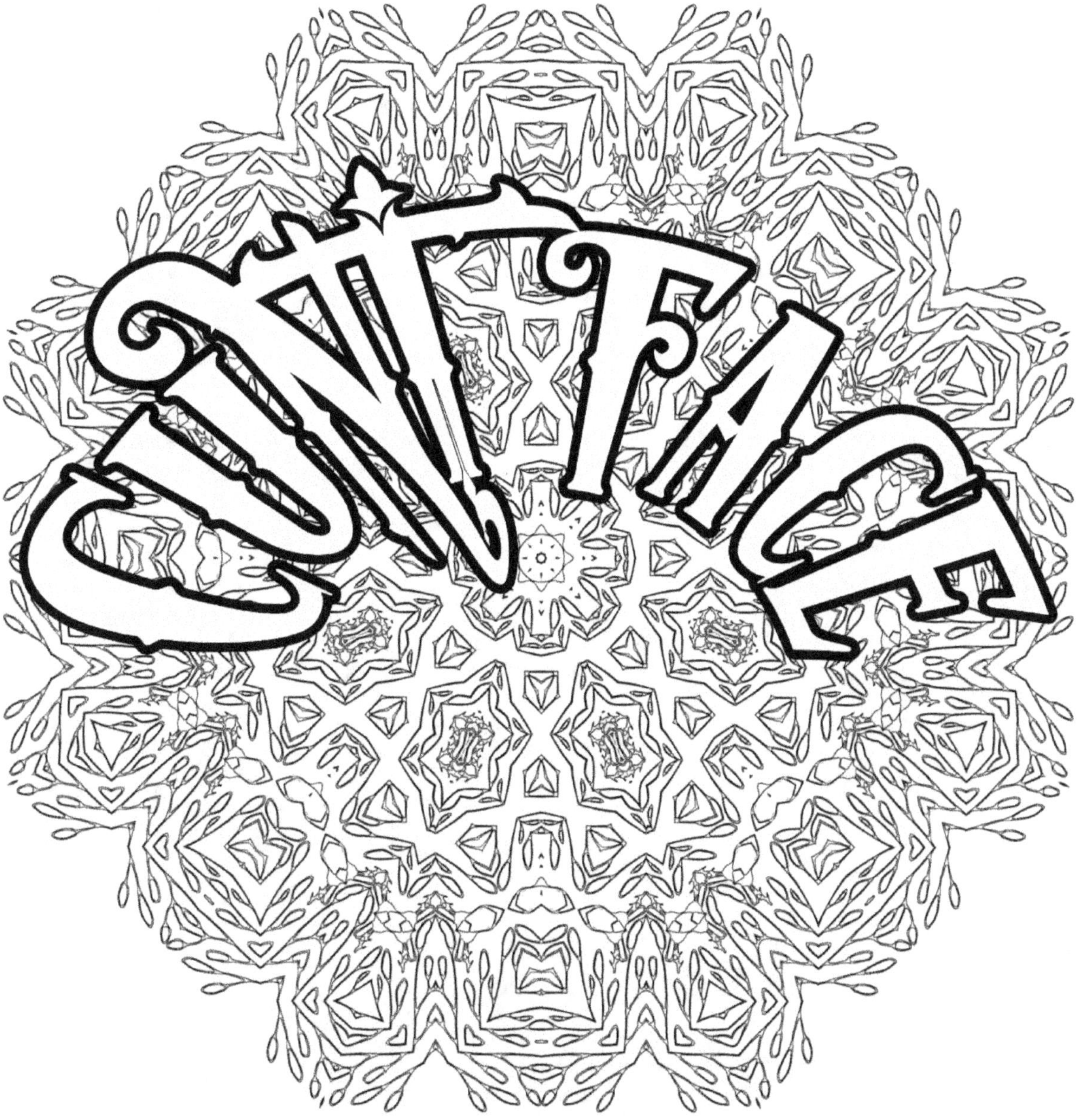

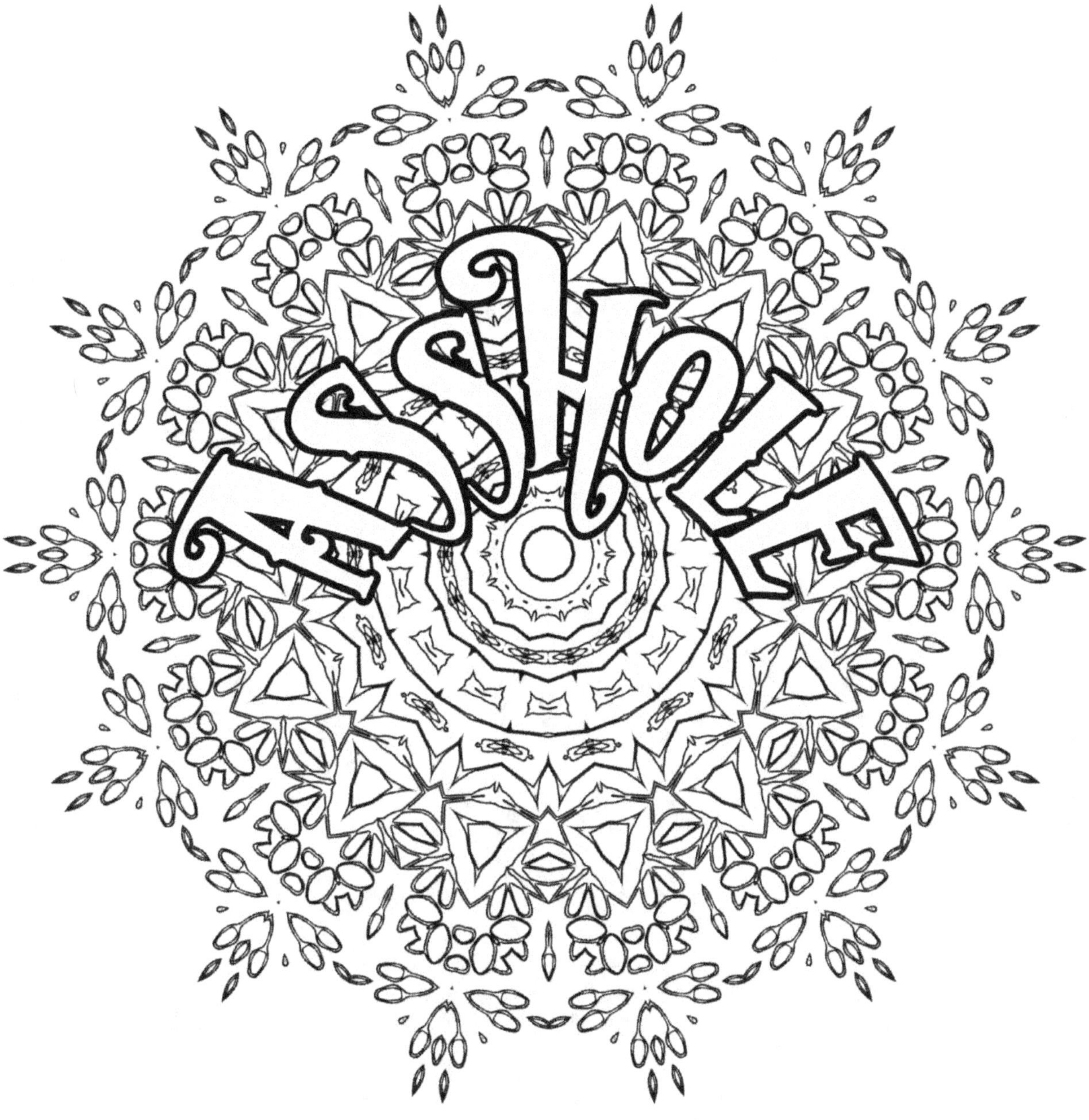
ASSHOLE

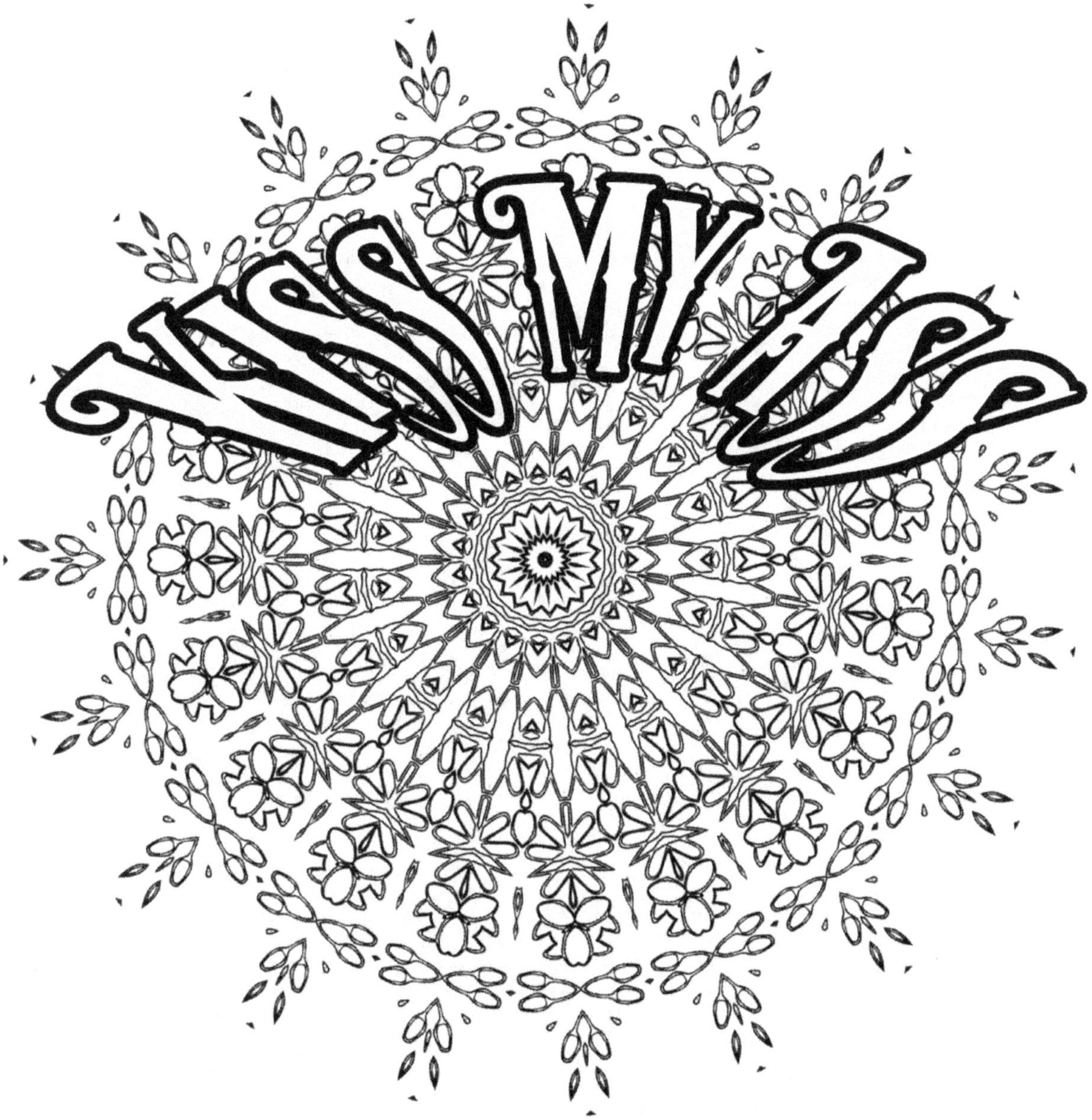
KISS MY ASS

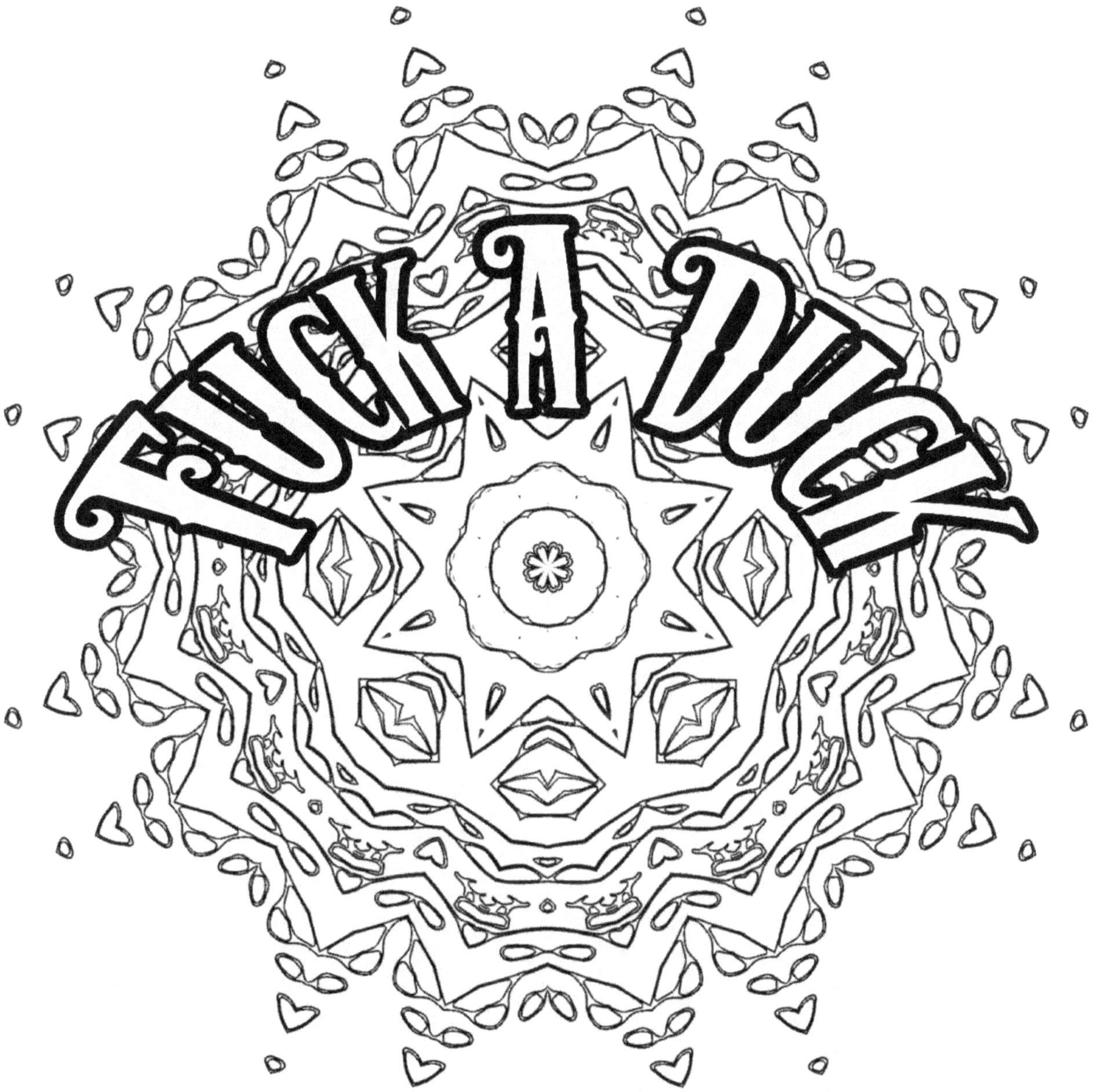
FUCK A DUCK

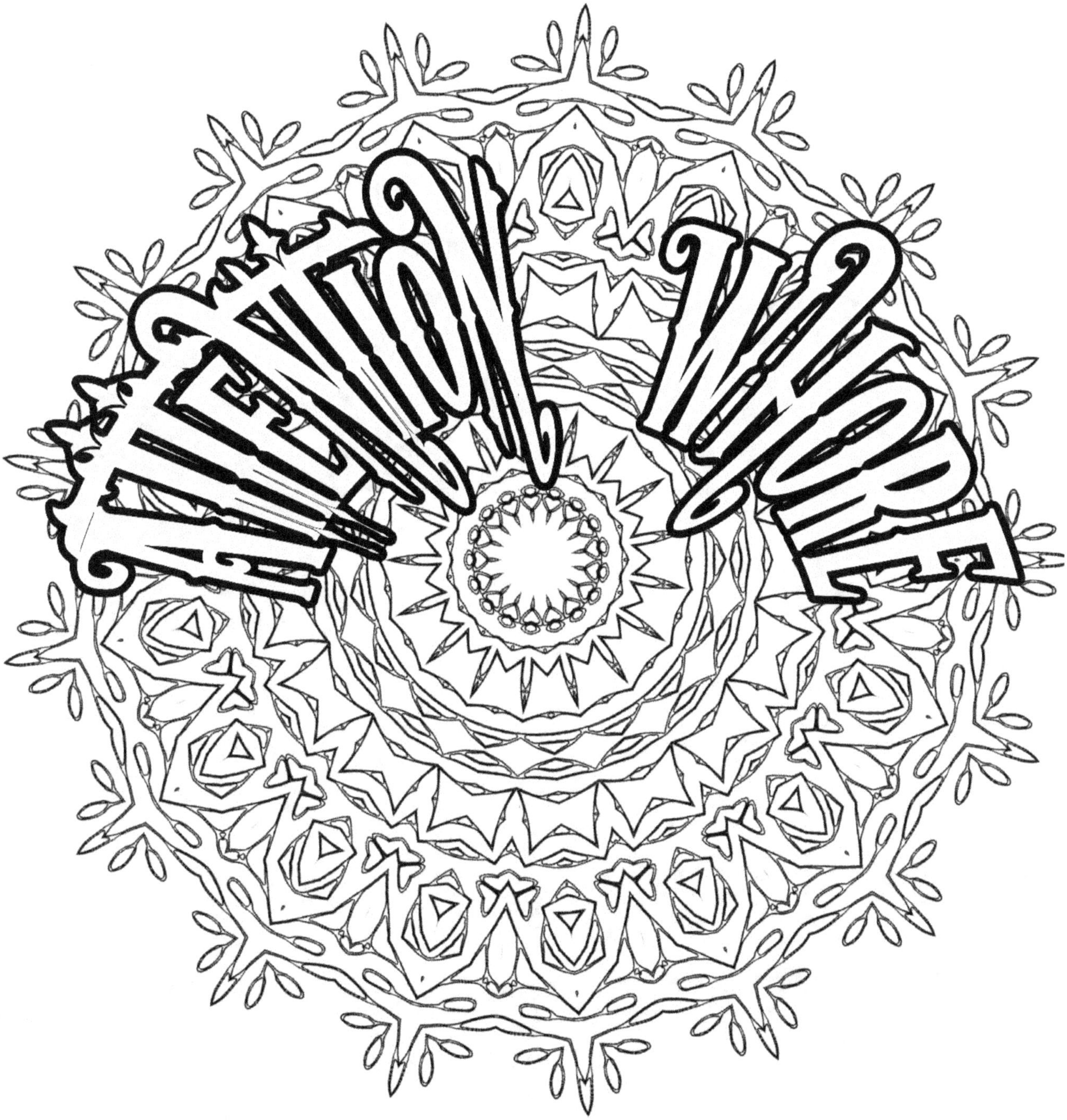
ATTENTION WHORE

www.ingramcontent.com/pod-product-compliance
Lightning Source LLC
Chambersburg PA
CBHW081749170526
45167CB00009B/3979
* 9 7 8 1 5 4 4 0 8 7 2 3 8 *